Tea and Inspiration

Mary Pielenz Hampton

Photography by Lorraine Maksoudian

A
JANET
THOMA
BOOK

THOMAS NELSON PUBLISHERS

Nashville • Atlanta • London • Vancouver

This book is lovingly dedicated to
Denis "G'pa" Hopson, my favorite Englishman.
Thank you for making a shy little girl feel smart.

Published in Nashville, Tennessee, by Thomas Nelson, Inc., Publishers, and distributed in Canada by Word Communications, Ltd., Richmond, British Columbia.

Published in association with the literary agency of Alive Communications, P.O. Box 49068, Colorado Springs, CO 80949.

Interior design by Steve Diggs & Friends, Nashville.

The Bible version used in this publication is THE NEW KING JAMES VERSION. Copyright © 1979, 1980, 1982, 1990, Thomas Nelson, Inc., Publishers.

Library of Congress Cataloging-in-Publication Data
Hampton, Mary Pielenz.
    Tea and inspiration: a collection of tea celebrations to share with your Lord and your loved ones / Mary Pielenz Hampton.
    p. cm.
    ISBN 0-7852-7704-8
    1. Women—prayer books and devotions—English. 2. Cookery (tea). I. Title.
BV4844.H27 1995
242'.643—dc20   95-11411
                                                                   CIP

2 3 4 5 6 — 00 99 98 97 96

Contents

Contents

Tea Celebrations for Special Occasions

Acknowledgments

After years of reading others' books, I only now understand how such a solitary occupation as writing a book can be so dependent upon so many people. This is my attempt to acknowledge the people in my life who have shared in creating this book.

Dean Hampton—my loving husband. Your encouragement and support combined with your great patience have lightened the burden and increased the rewards of this project—thank you.

My family—Family is unique among all other relationships in that each one's sorrow is the sorrow of all; each one's success the success of all. I'm happy to be able to share this with you.

Lorraine Maksoudian—It has been fun conceptualizing the photos and seeing them come to life through your camera. Thank you for your many contributions.

Kristine Peterson and the College Women's Bible study group—Thank you for all of your help and input and for being my "guinea pigs" for lessons and recipes.

Our Grace Church family—You will never fully understand what your love and support have meant to me over the years. Your influence and generosity can be seen throughout the pages of this book in many ways.

My "tea" friends over the years—Thank you for your friendship—I hope you will enjoy this tea "companion."

The many professionals at workshops and conferences that I've had the opportunity to learn from; David Kopp for illustrating the importance of personal transparency in my writing; J. B. Briggs for pointing out that it's never too late (or too soon) to make a dream come true. And of course, Greg Johnson of Alive Communications, Janet Thoma, and Emily Kirkpatrick at Thomas Nelson for seeing the merit in this project and helping me find my way through the publishing business.

Above all, I offer my thanks and praise to God: the Father, Creator of tea; the Holy Spirit, Author of inspiration; and my Lord Jesus Christ—as the apostle Paul put it, "I thank Christ Jesus our Lord, who has enabled me, because He counted me faithful, putting me into the ministry" (1 Tim. 1:12). Thank You for entrusting me with this book.

Preparing

for

Tea

Celebrations

Introduction

*T*he lace tablecloth flutters softly in the breeze from the open window as the sunshine glints off of Mother's favorite old cup and saucer. The room is perfumed with the scent of scones fresh from the oven. Daddy's big leather Bible is open to a favorite passage and the teakettle whistles that the celebration is about to begin.

Tea and Inspiration is a book that's intended to make spending time with the Lord a special occasion—just as though your dearest friend is coming to visit. Too often, we rush through our "quiet time" with the Lord, squeezing it in before the kids get up, between appointments, or just before we turn out the light. It is a rare occasion, often at a retreat or on vacation, when we take our Bible, find a comfortable, peaceful place, and invite our Lord to spend some special, uninterrupted, undistracted time alone with us.

It is my hope that this book will encourage you to take this kind of break every week or two and really share yourself with the Lord. Even Jesus took time apart from His ministry to go off alone and talk with His Father. How much more necessary it is that we spend this kind of time with God!

Tea and Inspiration is designed to encourage you to spend more intimate, truly special time alone with God and to give you a simple way to share with others in your life what you have learned in the process. Each devotional chapter contains a recipe, a corresponding Scripture passage, a meditation based on each passage, and usually, additional Scripture references for further study on the topic.

Each recipe has been chosen to represent the Scripture passage explained in that particular devotional message. God often used foods in feasts and festivals to remind His people, the Israelites, of messages or miracles. Our Creator used foods in this way because of the connection between the spirit and the body. The more senses that are touched in a learning experience, the more thoroughly the lesson is learned.

The Jewish people have celebrated the same feasts for thousands of years, using the same foods as a reminder of what the Lord has done for them. According to a Jewish friend of mine, during the Passover feast horseradish, or some other bitter herb, is eaten in memory of the bitterness of the bondage in Egypt; a mixture of honey, apples, and nuts represents the mortar that the Israelites used in building the pyramids in Egypt while in captivity; and unleavened bread signifies the haste with which they left Egypt. Jesus carried on this method of commemorating His teaching when He established Communion as a reminder of His sacrifice for us. In the same way, the recipes contained in this book can serve as an object lesson, a reminder of the lessons in God's Word each time you prepare them.

Jesus used His time alone with God to recharge, to be able to come back and face His disciples and the multitudes with renewed strength.

I've chosen teatime recipes for a couple of reasons. First, I love tea and its trappings and traditions. The recipes lend themselves well to pairings with Scripture passages. Second, there is a resurgence of the tradition of afternoon tea. It is a time to slow down and reflect on life. While you could microwave a cup of water and throw in a tea bag, a proper cup of tea can't be rushed—in the same way, our time with the Lord shouldn't be rushed.

In the preparation of each recipe, it is necessary to plan ahead—you need to be sure you have the required ingredients and the time to prepare the recipe. There is also the anticipation of the finished product, looking forward to sampling the new food and savoring the quiet time with the Lord. This type of planning adds to the expectation of the celebration that is to come.

After you have spent your special time with the Lord, enjoying the "fruits of your labor," the food can provide a simple, nonthreatening opening for you to share the truths you've learned with family or friends. Picture a plate of cookies shared with your children's playmates. As they enjoy the treat, you draw the parallel between the "rock cakes" and the pile of stones that Joshua and the nation of Israel erected to commemorate the Lord's faithfulness to them. Perhaps you have an unchurched neighbor who would enjoy your hospitality as you share your refreshments with her. How easy to mention that the cheese straws remind you of Moses' rod and how anything we surrender to God to use as He chooses can be filled with power beyond our wildest expectations.

The Scripture passage in each section is somewhat longer than what is usually included in a devotional or "meditation," but you are encouraged to have your Bible nearby so you can read the entire passage the devotion is based on. Following the Scripture is a meditation that contains my thoughts on the passage—what the Lord spoke to me. I hope it will be as though you and I are talking over a cup of tea. I'd love to hear how God has spoken to you, but since that isn't possible here and now, see what message He has for you and share that message with someone in your life.

It is my prayer that the Lord will be able to use the combination of the recipes and His Word to meet you exactly where you are and that you will go away from each time with Him refreshed, renewed, and ready to share what He's doing in your life.

Teatime Celebrations:
PAST, PRODUCTION, AND PREPARATIONS

*W*orldwide, more tea is consumed than any beverage other than water. While tea definitely had its beginnings in China, it is now a part of culture in both the Eastern and the Western worlds. The earliest records of tea date back to about 3000 B.C. when the Chinese used it primarily for medicinal purposes.

Tea eventually found its way to Japan, where the Japanese created a tea ceremony that is practiced still, a custom that ties every aspect of tea preparation into a spiritual experience.

As tea was discovered along the borders of Burma, the commissioner of Assam ordered that forests be cleared in order to plant tea. Portions of the lush hillsides of Darjeeling were planted as well, and the resulting Assam and Darjeeling teas are known as two of the finest teas available.

Dutch traders, commissioned by Queen Elizabeth, were the first to bring tea to Europe, and by the mid-1600s, tea had been added to the fare at English coffeehouses, advertised as a tonic for many ailments. It caught on quickly during this time, and tea accessories came into vogue. Even King Charles II had a collection of fine teacups, bowls, and serving pieces.

Anna, Duchess of Bedford, is credited with creating "afternoon tea" as a supplement to the usual British diet of a large breakfast and a moderate (often late) dinner with very little in between. Before long the idea caught on nationwide, and "teatime" was entrenched in British culture.

Teatime developed an etiquette all its own, with prescribed apparel—long flowing tea gowns—and expected fare including dainty sandwiches, sweets, and breads, all accompanied by fine tea. Tea was served using the finest china and linens the hostess had, and formal manners were the rule. There was even an unwritten list of appropriate and inappropriate topics for teatime conversation. Talk was light and inoffensive, although some juicy gossip—hence, "tea and scandal"—was not forbidden.

Often, for men who worked long days, tea sandwiches were packed up and sent along with them to the factories to sustain them until supper.

As the industrial world came of age, except for the upper classes, tea took on a more practical flavor. Dainty sandwiches were replaced by more substantial ones containing meat. The variety of sweets served wasn't as great, but they were ever-present.

In the twentieth century, afternoon tea has become less a tradition and more an occasion. It is not so often a meal as it is a party—or an excuse for one. Holding to tradition, even today's tea is not quite complete without scones, jam, and an assortment of delicacies. The ingredients and the preparation are generally simple, but the results are delicious and well worth the time to make them fresh.

AN ASSORTMENT OF TEAS

While tea is served in many forms and flavors, it all comes from the same plant, *Camellia sinensis*. The variations are a result of the differing soils and climates in the various tea-growing regions, as well as differences in processing. Nearly all tea is grown in the East, although there are small tea gardens in Argentina, Russia, and Kenya.

All true tea contains some level of caffeine. As a rule, the darker the tea, the more caffeine. The teas themselves differ according to the manner of processing. **Black** teas are fermented, which means the just-picked leaves have been left in a cool, damp place for several hours until they reach a certain color and pungency. The leaves are then *fired*—heated—to remove most of the moisture and stop the fermenting process. **Oolong** teas are semi-fermented. They are fired halfway through the usual fermenting stage, to prevent full fermentation. **Green** teas are handled in much the same way as the black tea, but they are heated after picking so that there is no fermenting process.

You've probably noticed that the tea section of the market contains varieties well beyond black, green, or oolong. The differences among them can be where they were grown, how they have been flavored, or what types of leaves have been blended. You might try the following:

Earl Grey (my favorite)—a black tea flavored with oil of bergamot, a small Mediterranean citrus fruit.

Keemun—the best China black tea; has a strong but pleasant flavor and is often used as a breakfast tea.

Lapsang Souchong—another tea from China; it gets its smoky flavor from being dried over pine fires; good with cheeses.

Formosa Oolong—the finest of the oolong teas; made in the same manner as others, but uses only the best quality leaves.

There are many other teas. It's an adventure worth undertaking to sample many varieties.

HERBAL TEAS

The term *herbal tea* is actually a misnomer. The truest tea producers and drinkers call the herbal drink an "infusion" because the water is infused with the herb. Herbal concoctions are often a combination of fruit or peels, flowers, leaves, herbs, and spices. While they are not actually tea, they are gaining in popularity because of the absence of caffeine in most varieties, as well as the great number of flavor possibilities.

PREPARING A PROPER CUP OF TEA

The most important element of a great cup of tea is the water. It should be fresh and cool, not having been boiled before. Water should be heated in a kettle on the stove to the boiling point.

While you wait for the water to boil, prepare the teapot by swirling hot water in it. This is important for a couple of reasons. First, temperature is essential to the tea releasing its flavor. If the water is cooled by being poured into a cold teapot, you won't achieve the fullest flavor. Second, the preheated teapot will retain the heat longer, so you can enjoy your fresh, hot tea to the bottom of the pot.

The tea can be placed directly in the teapot and strained as it is poured, or you can place the tea in an infuser, a sort of cage for the tea with fine holes to keep the leaves in. The amount of tea is commonly figured by using one teaspoon of tea per cup, and one for the pot. Allow the tea to steep for three to five minutes before pouring.

Use the time while the tea steeps to pull out your best cup and saucer, and place a fine plate and linen napkin on a tray. Add a cookie or two and a fresh flower if you have a garden, and prepare to enjoy a moment of calm in a world of chaos.

THE FINEST FOODS

Many of the foods traditionally associated with tea are from centuries-old recipes. I've selected some of them for this book, and in preparing them, I have learned a few things that will help make your tea a success every time.

The most important thing is to use the best ingredients you can. This does not necessarily mean the most expensive, just the freshest and most flavorful. If a recipe calls for butter but doesn't mention the option of margarine or shortening, by all means use real butter. In many of these dainties, butter is one of the primary flavors, and substituting can result in a very poor facsimile of the treat. My mother traditionally makes shortbread to give away during the holidays, and one especially budget-conscious year, she tried to save money by using margarine instead of butter. The results were so dreadful, she threw out the whole batch!

There are a few ingredients that are not common in most of our American kitchens but are readily available. You may want to take a look through the book and make note of items to add to your pantry. Among them are: dried currants; golden raisins; mixed, diced dried fruit; candied peel and glacé cherries; pecans; and almonds. Once you've acquired these items, you'll find that by and large the recipes are quite simple and definitely delicious.

Tea is all about enjoyment, relaxation, and taking the time to refresh your spirit.

Even though our kitchens have modernized a good deal since the inception of most of these recipes, I like the traditional preparation methods for these foods. It feels truer, somehow. You can experiment with using modern equipment, but a food processor just doesn't give the same texture to a dough as working in the butter with your hands.

Some shortcuts are worth taking, however. Store-bought pie crusts work beautifully for tarts and taste every bit as good as (and sometimes better than) the homemade variety. A can of chicken broth is a great substitute to boiling a chicken and reserving the liquid. A coffee grinder (well-cleaned, of course) is the best way to grind almonds, and if you can find almond paste, you can skip making it from scratch. Use whatever methods you are most comfortable with. Tea is all about enjoyment, relaxation, and taking the time to refresh your spirit.

How to Use This Book

There are many ways this book can be used. Please feel free to use any method that will make this an enriching experience for you.

My suggestion is for you to prepare the recipe ahead, then sit down with your treat and the book and have a special quiet time with the Lord. Most of the recipes can be made in advance, stored, and served later. You can prepare them whenever it's convenient and wait until you have a quiet moment to enjoy the whole experience. Of course, some of the recipes will taste best shortly after they are completed.

When I was growing up, I noticed that my mom often got the smallest piece of cake after she served everyone else. That didn't seem quite fair. With that in mind, these devotionals offer a chance for Mom to get the first and the best treat while celebrating her relationship with the Lord.

If you have a family, you could use this book as a basis for family devotions. Prepare the food in the evening, during nap time, or while the children are in school. Have your time with the Lord while Dad takes the kids to the park or while they play next door. Then share the experience with them when they get home.

It can be difficult to set aside cookies or some other treat without little fingers (or maybe not-so-little fingers) trying to snitch a sample here or there. But even very young children understand the concept of "company coming" and can accept that the treat can't be served until the company has arrived. It may take a time or two before they understand that this is for a special time for Mom and Jesus, and they will be able to share in it soon. You can tell the children that Jesus is coming on Saturday morning, and after He and Mom have had a chance to visit, the rest of the family will be able to join in. Children may even want to help prepare this special treat for their special guest.

Another way to make this kind of devotion work with children in the house is to set them up with a special "tea party" of their own while you have some time to yourself. Or perhaps you can show a new Bible-story video while you have your time with the Lord and then share the "tea party" with them when you've finished.

The book could also be used as a foundation or supplement for a ladies' Bible study group. Often a different person is responsible for refreshments each week. You could assign a different devotional and recipe to each person in the group and have her share the food and the lesson on her turn. Every few weeks you could have a special "review" for which all of the foods from the previous weeks are prepared. Review the lessons that accompanied each and discuss how the Lord has used them in your life.

I tested this concept on a college women's Bible study that I led. Each week I asked for one or two volunteers to prepare the refreshment for the following week. I used the passage of Scripture from the devotion as a jumping-off point for the Bible study, but expanded on it by including other passages that reinforced the message.

These are just a few suggestions. Be creative. See how many different ways you can incorporate this style of learning and sharing into your life.

So, whether you use your fine china or a secondhand teacup, your good napkins or a neatly folded paper towel, the finest tea you can find or a plain old tea bag, make this a beautiful experience—whatever beautiful is to you.

Tea

Celebrations

for Everyday

Occasions

Celebrating:
OUR HONOR IN CHRIST

Now it happened as they went that He entered a certain village; and a certain woman named Martha welcomed Him into her house. And she had a sister called Mary, who also sat at Jesus' feet and heard His word. But Martha was distracted with much serving, and she approached Him and said, "Lord, do You not care that my sister has left me to serve alone? Therefore tell her to help me."

And Jesus answered and said to her, "Martha, Martha, you are worried and troubled about many things. But one thing is needed, and Mary has chosen that good part, which will not be taken away from her."

LUKE 10:38–42

I would like to believe that I have a heart like Mary's, one that stops to listen to God whenever the opportunity arises. I am afraid though, that I probably come much closer to being like Martha. Hurrying about, planning, preparing, fixing, organizing, making lists, and worrying, *Will it all get done?* "It" can be my grocery shopping, the laundry, the meal for the potluck supper later on, the Bible study lesson, my latest craft project, etc., etc., etc.

These thoughts can overtake me during church, while having my devotions, in the midst of prayer—almost anywhere, the still, small voice of the Lord can get drowned out by the shouts of living in the sunset of the twentieth century.

I still believe that the planning, preparing, fixing, and organizing is important. I believe it is important to God. After all, I am trying to be faithful to do well the tasks He has set before me. I need to remember, though, that by far the most important thing I can do is to take the time to sit at Jesus' feet and really *listen.*

This invitation to listen to our Lord becomes even more precious when we realize that at the time Christ said this, women were not allowed to participate in this kind of religious discussion. This type of teaching was reserved for men only; Mary's participation would certainly not have been deemed "politically correct." It wasn't, in fact, until the twentieth century that Jewish women were allowed to participate in temple learning.

It is rather ironic, but all the more satisfying, to realize this in light of the world's perception that traditional Christianity seeks to "subjugate" women. Here is Jesus Christ, the center of our faith, throwing off tradition to elevate His beloved sisters and give them the opportunity for learning that other religious leaders denied them.

Don't you love this message? It is so good to know that Christ Himself has invited us to sit at His feet and learn directly from Him. And while it is good to be taught by learned men who can offer insights into the Scripture that we may not come across on our own, Jesus offers us a personal relationship—a friendship— with Him that is not dependent on anyone else, or even on what we do for Him.

This is the foundation for the rest of this book; that Jesus Christ loves you and has given you the opportunity to know Him personally, intimately. So, I hope you'll enjoy each of your special times with Him as you take your cup of tea, sit at the feet of Jesus, and open your heart to what He has to say to you.

. . . almost anywhere, the still, small voice of the Lord can get drowned out by the shouts of living in the sunset of the twentieth century.

For further examples of how Jesus treated women with honor, read the following passages:

- *John 8:1–11*   *The woman caught in adultery*
- *John 4:7–29*   *The woman at the well*
- *Mark 14:3–9*   *A woman anoints Jesus' feet*

Maids of Honor

The legend of these little tarts is that Henry VIII came upon the maids of his wife Catherine eating them. He liked them so much, he named them in the attendants' honor. I like the name because they remind me that our Lord treats all women as "maids of honor."

pastry, enough for
   one 9-inch pie
2 egg yolks
1/2 cup sugar
1/2 cup blanched ground almonds
   (almonds with no skin)

1 tbsp flour
1 tsp finely grated lemon
   peel or lemon zest
2 tbsp heavy (whipping)
   cream

Preheat oven to 400 degrees. Grease and flour muffin tins.

On a lightly floured surface, roll the pastry crust to about 1/4-inch thickness. Cut into 3-inch circles with a cookie cutter or the rim of a glass. Fit the rounds into the muffin tins, gently pressing the pastry dough to the sides. The pastry will be only about 1 inch deep. Gather the scraps into a ball and continue this until you've used it all. Set aside.

Filling: In a mixing bowl, lightly beat the egg yolks. Beat in the sugar, flour, almonds, and lemon peel. Slowly add the cream and beat until the mixture is smooth.

Carefully spoon about 1 tablespoon of the mixture into each pastry cup. (Some recipes call for dried currants to be placed on the top of each tart before baking; I like them as is.)

Bake for 15 to 20 minutes, until the filling is set and a light golden brown color. Carefully remove from the tins and place on a wire rack until completely cooled. Store in an airtight container.

Serve with Jasmine tea.

Celebrating:
Rock Collections

*T*hen Joshua called the twelve men whom he had appointed from the children of Israel, one man from every tribe; and Joshua said to them: "Cross over before the ark of the LORD your God into the midst of the Jordan, and each one of you take up a stone on his shoulder, according to the number of the tribes of the children of Israel, that this may be a sign among you when your children ask in time to come, saying, 'What do these stones mean to you?' Then you shall answer them that the waters of the Jordan were cut off before the ark of the covenant of the LORD; when it crossed over the Jordan, the waters of the Jordan were cut off. And these stones shall be for a memorial to the children of Israel forever."

FROM JOSHUA 3:10–4:24

I think God is especially aware of our human tendency toward forgetfulness. Maybe that's why He established so many traditions for the Israelites to follow. The Bible is full of feasts and festivals that the Lord established for Israel so that they would remember His works.

I think that's why He directed them to take stones from the bottom of the Jordan river as they passed through it. Sure, it was partly for future generations to have a tangible memento of this tremendous miracle. But it was also a reminder to the people who were there at the time. Even though it was not commonplace for the waters of a river at flood stage to stack up and create a dry passing, time passes and memories fade, and the miracle could begin to seem like a dream even to eyewitnesses.

We're still like that today. We pray, maybe for a miracle, maybe just for an answer. No sooner does the prayer escape from "our lips to God's ears" before we've forgotten that we prayed at all. This by itself isn't so bad. Maybe it implies a great faith—we trust that our prayer will be answered, so we don't need to keep checking on it. The problem is, it often means that we don't recognize answered prayer when it occurs. We need a way to commemorate those answers.

Hannah Hurnard illustrates this concept beautifully in her classic allegory *Hind's Feet on High Places*. The main character, Much Afraid, is on a journey to the "High Places" where "perfect love casteth out fear." Along the way, she learns many lessons about surrendering to the Chief

Shepherd, and she commemorates each one by taking a special stone from the site and keeping it in a bag. At times the stones seem like useless baggage. Yet she remembers the promises that each one signifies, and they give her strength and the encouragement she needs to continue on her journey.[1]

Do you remember those days of childhood when a rock picked up on a family outing or a shell from a trip to the shore had great meaning? As a child, did you have one of those shoe boxes filled with odds and ends, a "collection" that no one else saw any value in? You could explain each item though, couldn't you?

Do you have a system for commemorating significant events in your life now? It might be a scrapbook, a memory box, a journal. I think we need to extend this practice into our spiritual lives—a collection of "stones" to help us through those hard times when the Shepherd is out of sight and our own thoughts and fears seek to keep us from continuing along the path before us.

Start your own collection of spiritual mementos. No matter how simple, as your collection grows, you'll see how abundantly faithful our God is. Make a ceremony of adding to your collection. Bake a batch of the "rock cakes," explain what the Lord has done, and then add the memento to your collection. If you have children, you may be surprised at how they will look for opportunities to add to the collection themselves.

Later, when the road ahead seems to lead down to places of desolation rather than to the High Places, you can take out your mementos and see how far the Lord has led you and trust that He still knows the best path for your future.

For more about feasts, festivals, and other commemorations in Scripture, see:

- *Exodus 23:14–19*   *Feasts*
- *Mark 14:22–25*   *Communion*
- *John 4:1–2*   *Baptism*

Rock Cakes

These cookies got their name because they look like rocks—not because they taste like them! Share them as a reminder not to forget the path the Lord has taken you down or the things He's taught you along the way.

2 cups flour
1 tbsp baking powder
1/2 cup sugar
1/2 cup (1 stick) butter or margarine, softened
2 eggs, beaten
3 tbsp milk
1 cup currants

Preheat oven to 350 degrees. Grease a cookie sheet. Mix flour, baking powder, and sugar together. With fingers, rub in butter or margarine until mixture resembles coarse bread crumbs. Mix in currants, add beaten eggs and milk, and mix to form a stiff batter.

Spoon mixture onto greased cookie sheet and bake for about 15 minutes, until tops are golden. Remove from cookie sheet and cool on a wire rack. Store in an airtight container.

Rock cakes would be great with any of your favorite teas.

Celebrating:
THE DESIRES OF YOUR HEART

At Gibeon the LORD appeared to Solomon in a dream by night; and God said, "Ask! What shall I give you?" And Solomon said . . . "Now, O LORD my God, You have made Your servant king instead of my father David, but I am a little child; I do not know how to go out or come in . . . Therefore give to Your servant an understanding heart to judge Your people, that I may discern between good and evil. For who is able to judge this great people of Yours?"
Then God said to him: "Because you have asked this thing . . . see, I have given you a wise and understanding heart, so that there has not been anyone like you before you, nor shall any like you arise after you. And I have also given you what you have not asked: both riches and honor . . ."
Then Solomon awoke; and indeed it had been a dream.

FROM 1 KINGS 3:5–15

*H*ave you ever noticed that in that drowsy haze between being asleep and being awake, your deepest thoughts seem to drift to the surface? In the first blush of a new relationship, thoughts of the beloved; in difficult times, your most disturbing troubles; when faced with a new challenge, anxious anticipation.

When unencumbered by the conscious mind that often suppresses our most intense feelings, our subconscious mind lets loose what is hidden in our hearts. As the transition between wakefulness and sleep passes into dreaming, those thoughts often become a mini-drama—color, sound, and motion coming together behind our closed eyes to express our most heartfelt longings and concerns.

I often wish I could attach a recorder of some sort to these thoughts. In that twilight fog, many brilliant lines have been composed, many problems have been solved, and countless plans have been devised, only to evaporate with the morning light.

In spite of what we hear to the contrary, in general we can't control our dreams. While they may be based on what has been on our minds or in our hearts, the outcome is usually not something we can manipulate in our sleep. Have you ever had a dream where someone made you mad or hurt your feelings, and you woke up carrying that feeling around with you? That's an indication to me that while we may provide our subconscious with the subject matter, our dreams can have a life of their own, sometimes expressing what we have buried deep inside.

This is why I am so impressed that Solomon asked for wisdom and discernment when God was there offering to fulfill any desire. Solomon was so humbled by the position he was in that even in his sleep, his greatest wish was to be equipped to lead God's people in the way God wanted.

". . . give to Your servant an understanding heart to judge Your people, that I may discern between good and evil. For who is able to judge this great people of Yours?"

What would you ask for if God offered you anything you desired? Would you ask for long life or riches or protection for those you love? Would you ask for wisdom or a deeper relationship with Him? When your wakeful mind isn't alert to tell you what you *should* ask for, would your unconscious heart ask for something that would please God?

Psalm 37, a psalm of David, tells us that if we delight ourselves in the Lord, He will give us the desires of our heart. Some people have said that this means that if we are seeking the Lord first, our desires will conform to His. I like to think that it actually means that God places the desires there to begin with. But either way, at the center of having a heart like Solomon's, a heart that seeks godly wisdom even in sleep, is seeking first after God. And as Matthew 6:33 tells us, as we do seek Him, "all these things shall be added to you." Just like Solomon, God promises you and me that seeking after Him with our whole heart will open the doors of His grace to us.

For more on seeking Him first read:
- *Proverbs 8:17*
- *Luke 11:10*
- *Colossians 3:1–2*

Dream Cookies

These are light, crisp cookies that are easy to prepare—and the recipe requires no eggs. Serve these when you need a reminder that God wants to give us the desires of our heart—we just need to seek Him wholeheartedly.

1 cup (2 sticks) butter, soft but not melted
3/4 cup granulated sugar
1/2 tsp orange or almond extract
2 cups all-purpose flour
1 tsp baking powder
blanched almonds, halves or slivers

Preheat oven to 300 degrees. In medium bowl, use mixer on medium speed to beat butter, sugar, and extract together until light and fluffy.

In a separate bowl, sift together flour and baking soda. Add dry ingredients to butter mixture until well blended and smooth.

If dough is too soft or sticky to handle, cover with plastic wrap and refrigerate for about an hour, or until dough is firm.

Form dough into 1-inch balls, about 1/2 tablespoon of batter each. Place on ungreased cookie sheet, leaving room for cookies to spread.

Press almond half or sliver into top of each ball, flattening it slightly. Bake for 25 minutes or until lightly golden brown. Cool on a wire rack.

These cookies are delicious with Darjeeling tea.

Celebrating:

FREEDOM FROM BONDAGE

Now the mixed multitude who were among them yielded to intense craving; so the children of Israel also wept again and said: "Who will give us meat to eat? We remember the fish which we ate freely in Egypt, the cucumbers, the melons, the leeks, the onions, and the garlic; but now our whole being is dried up; there is nothing at all except this manna before our eyes!"

NUMBERS 11:4–6

The Israelites may have been freed from the bondage of their slavery in Egypt, but they carried a different bondage in their hearts—a bondage of spirit. This bondage is far worse than a lack of physical freedom because it interferes with God's blessings flowing freely to us.

In obedience and trust there are blessings of peace and contentment that God can provide no matter what our physical circumstances. Israel showed that they didn't really trust God to keep His Word and bring them the blessings He wanted to give them. They complained because they were in captivity, then they complained because they had such a long journey ahead. First they didn't have meat, then they had so much it made them sick. They spoke as though they would trade their freedom to be back on Pharaoh's construction crews if they could just have some leeks and melons to eat!

Jonah is another example of someone who appeared to be free but was actually in a bondage of his own creation. Jonah was told that the Lord wanted him to go to Nineveh. Nineveh was sinning and the Lord wanted them to return to Him. Jonah hated the Ninevites and would just as soon let them perish.

Jonah headed in the opposite direction, but the misfortune he encountered along the way led him back to complete the mission God had for him. God's expectations never changed. He saw to it that Jonah carried out His plan, but Jonah had thwarted God's blessings by being defiant.

Unfortunately, the shortsightedness and ingratitude of Israel and Jonah can follow us today. We pray for God's provision, for His will for our lives, for opportunities to serve Him or to share the gospel, but when we get what we ask for, we also want to set the terms.

In obedience and trust there are blessings of peace and contentment that God can provide no matter what our circumstances.

"I'll serve You in California but not in Kansas" (or maybe the other way around).

"I'll share the gospel with my closest neighbor but not my closest family members."

"I'll give You a tenth of all I have if You can see to it that I have (*fill in the blank*)."

One of the great blessings of having the Word of God is being able to look at those who have gone before us and learn from their mistakes. By looking at Jonah and the children of Israel, we can see that desiring what is out of God's plan is actually desiring to remain in bondage to our old ways and our selfish ambition. That can keep us from attaining God's plan and His blessing for our lives.

If we will trust God to keep His promises and follow His leading, God will provide all that we need and often even more than we ask.

The rest of the story about Jonah can be found in the book of Jonah. Israel's experiences while in captivity in Egypt are recounted in Exodus, chapters 5 through 14.

Leek and Bacon Knots

This savory dinner roll reminds me that it is important not to seek after things that God doesn't have in His plan. The Israelites remembered the meat and the leeks that they had while in Egypt but overlooked the bondage they were in at that time. These leek and bacon knots can help us remember that mere bread from the Lord's hand is far better than the sweetest treat that takes us away from His plan.

2 tbsp butter or olive oil	2 cups warm (120 degrees) water
1 leek, finely chopped	2 cups all-purpose flour
6 ounces bacon, chopped	2 cups whole wheat flour
1 tbsp active dry yeast	2 tsp salt
1/2 tsp granulated sugar	2 tsp butter

Grease two baking sheets. Cook leek in butter or oil until soft. Remove leek from skillet and drain on paper towels. Cook chopped bacon until slightly crisp. Set bacon aside to cool with leek.

Mix yeast, sugar, and water and set in a warm place for a few minutes until foamy and increased in volume.

Sift flour and salt together into a large bowl. Rub in butter with hands. Stir in cooled leek and bacon. Add yeast mixture and mix until it forms a stiff dough. Turn onto a floured board and knead for about 10 minutes. Dough should be smooth and elastic.

Place dough in a large oiled bowl, cover with a towel or plastic, and leave in a warm place for 90 minutes or until doubled.

Preheat oven to 425 degrees. Remove cover from dough, punch dough down, and knead for two to three minutes. Divide into twelve equal pieces, and roll each into a rope about twelve inches long. Tie each strip of dough into a knot and place on a greased baking sheet. Allow to rise again for 30 minutes or until double.

Brush tops of rolls with beaten egg for shine. Bake for 15 minutes or until golden. Cool on wire rack. These rolls make a meal when served with split-pea soup. (Very good with any oolong tea.)

Celebrating:
BUSYNESS

Who can find a virtuous wife?
For her worth is far above rubies. . . .
She watches over the ways of her household,
And does not eat the bread of idleness.
Her children rise up and call her blessed;
Her husband also, and he praises her:
"Many daughters have done well,
But you excel them all."
Charm is deceitful and beauty is passing,
But a woman who fears the LORD, she shall be praised.
Give her of the fruit of her hands,
And let her own works praise her in the gates.

FROM PROVERBS 31:10, 26–31

The Proverbs 31 woman. Which of us doesn't envy her glowing description even while we resent the lofty example we feel we could never attain?

We look at the list of accomplishments of this (fictional) woman and think "I could never do *all* of that!" Who could? And yet, when the list is broken down one by one, we find we are capable of many of the items on the list. The rest we probably could do, given time and training.

So what stops us?

Idleness. Or a less polite but more descriptive term—laziness. The way I see it, the key to this woman of honor is in verse 27: "[She] does not eat the bread of idleness."

Idleness can come in many forms. I have an idea that we all have our pet idlenesses. Sometimes they can even be disguised as something good, but in our heart of hearts, we know it's idleness just the same.

Television is the most obvious and probably the most often targeted. It really is easy to lose yourself in some program or other, only to find that hours have slipped away without accomplishing anything productive.

My biggest vice for many years (after my parents got rid of the television) was reading. That doesn't sound so bad; after all, reading is a good thing. I even won an award in a junior high read-a-thon. And while it's generally agreed that reading what my friend Renee calls "trashy romance novels" isn't the best use of our time, it is possible to read even "good" books or magazines to such an extent that we neglect other things that need to be done.

We may turn down opportunities to serve others because we "don't have the time." Or maybe we shut out family members while we're absorbed in our latest read. Maybe the material itself fills our heads with "possibilities" that lead us to ignore the realities of the life right in front of us.

Idleness can also come in the form of socializing. Whether over the phone or over tea, it's easy to spend so much time talking that dinner gets started late, or the laundry doesn't get done, or the checkbook doesn't get balanced (and that little math error made last week turns into a major budget crisis).

Idleness is something I've always struggled with, but this isn't all as discouraging as it may sound. I think God just wants us to be balanced in our lives—in our work and in our play.

There are many ways to become more productive. Set time limits on your "pleasure" reading. If there's a TV program you really want to see, clip coupons or fold laundry while you watch. Put an extra-long cord on the phone so that time spent catching up with a dear friend can also be used to cook dinner or iron clothes.

The challenge is to look at the idleness in our lives and see how it can be overcome. For me it is a continuous struggle, but success along the way makes the struggle worth it. And one of the benefits along the way is knowing that our time is being used well and that we have no need for excuses or explanations. As we begin to achieve this balance in our lives, our works will "praise [us] in the gates" and the praise and respect of our family and those we serve will follow.

Some other Scriptures that offer thoughts on idleness:
- *Proverbs 6:6–11; 10:4*
- *Ecclesiastes 10:18*

Scones

Scones are the simplest and most common of the traditional tea breads. I like to think that the Proverbs 31 woman might eat this "bread of industriousness." Just taking the time to make the scones can help remind us not to "eat the bread of idleness."

2 cups all-purpose flour
1 tbsp baking powder
1 1/2 tbsp sugar
1/4 cup (1/2 stick) butter, chilled
2/3 cup milk

Preheat oven to 425 degrees. Butter a baking sheet.

Sift together flour, baking powder, and sugar. With hands, rub butter into dry ingredients until it resembles coarse bread crumbs.

Add milk, mixing after first 1/3 cup, adding remaining milk a little at a time, if needed. Blend together just until ingredients form a ball. Dough should be stiff and not sticky.

Turn dough onto a floured board and gently knead into a round, about 1 inch thick. Slice dough into eight equal wedges and place 1 inch apart on greased baking sheet, or cut into rounds using 3-inch glass or cookie cutter.

Bake 10 to 12 minutes or until golden brown. Serve hot from the oven with jam and whipped cream.

I like scones with any floral-blend tea, like rose or chrysanthemum. One Scandinavian blend I found contains marigold and cornflowers.

Tips: For best results, don't overmix or knead dough too long. If you want to prepare scones ahead, mix dry ingredients and set aside. Add milk and shape immediately before baking; or mix together and cut into shapes, then freeze the dough until you're ready to bake.

Variations: Before adding milk, mix in 1/3 cup of one of these items: raisins, currants, dried cranberries, mixed dried fruit, chopped dates, or pecans.

Celebrating:
A ROCKY PATH

*N*ow they departed and came back to Moses and Aaron
. . . and said: "We went to the land where you sent us. It
truly flows with milk and honey, and this is its fruit.
Nevertheless the people who dwell in the land are strong;
the cities are fortified and very large; moreover we saw the
descendants of Anak there." . . . But Joshua the son of
Nun and Caleb the son of Jephunneh spoke to all the con-
gregation of the children of Israel, saying: "The land we
passed through to spy out is an exceedingly good land. If
the LORD delights in us, then He will bring us into this
land and give it to us, 'a land which flows with milk and
honey.' Only do not rebel against the LORD, nor fear the
people of the land, for they are our bread; their protection
has departed from them, and the LORD is with us.
Do not fear them."

FROM NUMBERS 13:23–14:9

he Lord promised Israel a land of their own. A land "flowing with milk and honey." What He didn't promise them, however, was a smooth, paved road free from obstacles.

Jesus gave us the same kind of promise when He said, "These things I have spoken to you, that in Me you may have peace. In the world you will have tribulation; but be of good cheer, I have overcome the world" (John 16:33).

It is easy to look at the obstacles the world puts up around us and to feel that there is no point in fighting the battles ahead. I think this is true of this period of time in American history more than any in the past.

During my senior year of high school, my parents were led by God to enter a "land flowing with milk and honey" to establish a rescue mission. The "land" was a beautiful little town on the coast of California. At that time, there was no accommodation for the homeless.

Trying to get the work established was like trying to conquer a land of giants.

Giant number 1: a city council who didn't want to "give transients a reason to stay in town."

Giant number 2: a historical home preservation group who didn't want a shelter in a Victorian home in the center of town.

Giant number 3: a group of parents concerned about bringing "those people" to a place half a block from an elementary school.

Giant number 4: previous tenants of the leased house, who hadn't moved out before we arrived. They didn't believe things would work out, so they planned to wait it out.

The obstacles weren't removed. But the Lord honored His promise to "make [their] feet like deer's feet" (Hab. 3:19). The Christian Hope Center was established by God creating a path that allowed free movement among and around the obstacles.

Giant number 1 was tamed when a growing national concern for the homeless situation prompted members of our community to take up the cause and support the idea of an emergency family shelter.

Giant number 2 joined our side of the battle when my sister became friends with the daughter of the president of the neighborhood preservation group. As this friend's mother became better acquainted with our family and the goals of the Christian Hope Center, she too spoke in favor of the project.

Giant number 3 was quieted by the rules that were established for our guests. There was no opportunity for loitering or disturbing the school or the children. This giant was slain a short time after the work got under way when the city decided it didn't need to use the elementary school site any longer.

Giant number 4 finally was moved out when they saw that our God was bigger than the city council and all the other giants and that the Christian Hope Center was going to operate as planned.

Are there giants in your land? Is the path ahead filled with rocks and rough spots? Looking forward can be intimidating, and it can be tempting to turn back or stay put. But the journey can be more interesting, and the hand of God more evident, because of what it takes to get to the destination. May we always look for God's path rather than the road free from obstacles.

For more about how the Lord helped others move forward on roads filled with obstacles, read:

- *1 Samuel 19 and 24*
- *Nehemiah 1–7*

Milk and Honey Bread

Just as the Lord promised Israel a "land flowing with milk and honey," this bread flows with milk and honey. It is topped with a path of sweetness encrusted with boulders of pecans as a reminder that the road to God's plan for us is often paved with obstacles, but encountering them makes the trip richer.

3/4 cup milk	*Topping:*
3/4 cup honey	1 cup sifted powdered sugar
3 tbsp butter, cut in pieces	1/4 tsp vanilla
2 1/2 cups flour	1 tbsp milk
1 tbsp baking powder	1/4 cup pecan pieces
1/2 cup sugar	
1/2 tsp salt	

Preheat oven to 350 degrees (325 degrees if using a glass baking dish). Grease a 9-inch loaf pan.

In a small saucepan, combine milk, honey, and butter. Stir over low heat until honey is dissolved and butter is melted and blended with milk. Pour into a large mixing bowl and cool to room temperature.

In a medium bowl, sift together flour, sugar, baking powder, and salt.

After honey mixture is cooled, add flour mixture and stir just until well blended. Do not overmix. Pour into pan, and bake 60 minutes or until cake tester inserted in center comes out clean.

Topping: Mix powdered sugar, vanilla, and milk. Blend until a thick glaze is formed. (Add additional milk 1/2 teaspoon at a time, if needed.)

After bread is cooled, spread glaze across top, then sprinkle with chopped pecans. Allow glaze to set an hour or two before slicing.

Serve with black tea sweetened with milk and honey.

Celebrating:
ABUNDANT GIVING

"To the Glory of God"

Now Jesus sat opposite the treasury and saw how the people put money into the treasury. And many who were rich put in much. Then one poor widow came and threw in two mites, which make a quadrans. So He called His disciples to Himself and said to them, "Assuredly, I say to you that this poor widow has put in more than all those who have given to the treasury; for they all put in out of their abundance, but she out of her poverty put in all that she had, her whole livelihood."

MARK 12:41–44

*I*n the village of Cornish, New Hampshire, the late afternoon sun cast long shadows on the road as Sally Thomas hurried toward town. The cold gray bricks of the Congregational Church were bathed in the golden glow of the setting sun. She was grateful to the Chase family for the afternoon off. "They're such good people," she thought. "I have been very blessed to be employed by a family who loves the Lord as they do." Even though her wages were small, less than fifty cents a week, the Chases provided food to sustain her and a room to protect her. And it was so exciting to be a part of the church in "the New World" and to help with the work they were doing overseas. She really didn't need much else.

Sally loved to come to the church all alone like this. In the silence, she could feel the Lord's presence as she pulled open the heavy oak doors. Even though the ornate stained-glass windows let in little of the waning sunlight, the joy she brought with her illuminated the tiny foyer.

The coins she dropped into the offering box echoed as they landed on its empty bottom. Sally liked the sound. She liked to think that the big noise the tiny coins made was the Lord magnifying her gift.

Even though her gifts weren't large by some standards, giving all she had made her feel significant in God's eyes. She almost always gave in secret like this. At times, it was uncomfortable, having so little to offer. Those who gave much were often made much of, even in the church. But it thrilled her heart to be able to give what she did have to the Lord's work.[2]

Like the widow and her mites, Sally Thomas has been recorded in church history for her giving heart. Sally didn't know that the son of her minister would record her generosity for people two centuries in the future to see. The widow didn't know her story would be recorded in Scripture. They didn't give what they did because someone was watching. Both women gave from a pure heart.

It is hard to imagine being generous of spirit to the point of giving our whole livelihood to the church—or to any other "good cause" for that matter. Someone put it this way: "The problem with our giving is that we give the widow's mite, but not with the widow's spirit."

Have you ever wondered why the widow had so little? If God knew her heart and how generous she was, couldn't she have accomplished even more if she was given more? I think God allowed her to have exactly what she needed to accomplish His purpose for her life. I think He still does that.

It's not by chance that I was born in Lansing, Michigan, rather than in the jungles of Ecuador or some other country. It was no fluke that I had the opportunity to be educated. Nor was it simply coincidence that my mother consistently took us to church and that I came to know the Lord at an early age. God chose me to be born in America, to be educated, to know Him. I can best be used by Him right where I am, with the opportunities and gifts He has provided me. If I compare myself to others who seem to have so much more than me, it's easy to overlook the abundance that God has given to me.

I think God has placed each of us just where we can best accomplish His work. We may not feel rich, but we don't have to wait until we have a certain amount of money or education or experience to be used by God. As we give out of our poverty—poverty of pocket, poverty of spirit, or poverty of experience—the Lord will bless our offerings and magnify them to His glory.

To see more of how God can magnify small offerings, read: Matthew 14:13–21; and 1 Samuel 17:1–51.

Cheese Pennies

These simple but flavorful little crackers are a reminder that the Lord can use what we give Him out of our poverty even more than a great amount given out of our abundance.

2 cups (about 16 ounces) finely grated cheddar cheese
   (any sharpness)
1 cup (2 sticks) butter, room temperature
2 cups flour
1 tsp salt
1 tsp paprika
1/4 tsp cayenne pepper

In a medium bowl, cream butter until fluffy. Add grated cheese and blend together well. Sift together dry ingredients. Add to cheese mixture a little at a time, mixing until a stiff dough is formed.

Shape into logs about 1 inch in diameter. Place on waxed paper. To slice into "pennies," use dental floss or thread. Slide under log, wrap ends over top of log and pull, slicing through.

Gather pennies back into log shapes or place on a plate and cover with foil. Refrigerate overnight or freeze for a time before baking. (They will bake more evenly if all the ingredients have reached the same temperature.)

Place on an ungreased baking sheet and bake in a 375 degree oven for 10 to 12 minutes. Cool on a wire rack, and store in an air-tight container.

The dough will freeze well for baking at a later time. Cheese pennies are a treat for brown-bag lunches in place of chips.

Celestial Seasonings makes a Vanilla Maple tea that is really good with these.

Celebrating:
GOD'S APPROVAL

And the LORD said to Moses, "Go, get down!
*For your people whom you brought out of the land
of Egypt have corrupted themselves. They have made
themselves a molded calf, and worshiped it and
sacrificed to it, and said, 'This is your god, O Israel,
that brought you out of the land of Egypt!'" . . .
So Moses' anger became hot . . . then he took the
calf which they had made, burned it in the fire,
and ground it to powder; and he scattered it on
the water and made the children of Israel drink it.
And Moses said to Aaron, "What did this people do to
you that you have brought so great a sin upon them?"
So Aaron said, "You know the people, that they
are set on evil. For they said to me,
'Make us gods that shall go before us.'"*

FROM EXODUS 32:1–24

I don't think Aaron intended to be disobedient. He just wanted to keep the people from grumbling. Ask any leader—the worst part of the job is doing your best and getting nothing but complaints for all your efforts.

It's easy to look at Aaron and say, "How could you give in that way?" Aaron knew what God expected, but the people grumbled, and he was right there with a plan of action to make them happy. He was more interested in keeping the people from speaking against him than in pleasing the Lord.

But can't you relate to Aaron just a little bit? After all, don't we all want to please the people in our life? Our boss. Our spouse. Our parents. Our kids. The people at church. The list goes on and on. Sometimes it's just easier to go after the approval of the people we can see than it is to do what the Lord has asked of us.

Before Dean and I were engaged, we were discussing our plans and our vision for the future. Dean is preparing for the ministry, and at that time I was very excited about my own career and some new opportunities that had come my way. I was struggling with the idea of staying home full-time once we had children.

"It's important to me that the family be the first priority," Dean said.

"But how happy will the family be if I'm miserable because all I do is cook, clean, and baby-sit? That's not enough for me," I whined in response.

It made perfect sense to me. I know that raising a family is very important, but there is very little in the way of admiration and approval to go along with the long hours and hard work. A part of me really thrives on the approval and accolades that come from a job well done. And to me, that job had to be outside the home.

Dean was concerned and went to our pastor to seek his guidance. Pastor Keller asked, "Whose approval is Mary really seeking?" Although it was hard for me to face, I knew that in my heart I was more interested in pleasing the people I worked with and having their approval than I was in doing what God asked me to do.

Scripture contains many examples of people who honored God first and were in turn honored by the people around them. One of the best examples is Daniel. A young Israelite taken into captivity in Babylon, Daniel "purposed in his heart that he would not defile himself" (Dan. 1:8), and he won the approval of the man in charge of him. As Daniel was faithful to keep his commitments to the Lord, he was given the opportunity to serve the king. The king saw that Daniel's discernment was above all of the advisers and sorcerers he employed. Daniel ultimately became a trusted adviser to the king.

The important thing in this case is that Daniel was obedient because it was the right thing to do. His request not to eat the food from the king's table and his faithfulness in prayer even after prayer was outlawed could have resulted in his death. He didn't have self-serving motives of glory and honor, yet God chose to honor him. And even as God honored Daniel, He had a purpose that Daniel would bring greater glory to Him.

The main difference between Aaron and Daniel is that Aaron became *distracted* by his circumstances but Daniel kept his focus on God *despite* the circumstances. Our first priority needs to be to do whatever the Lord has instructed each of us to do. It is the Lord's approval we must seek first. He will meet all our other needs.

More about how Daniel sought God's approval can be found in Daniel, chapters 1 and 2.

Grapefruit Barley Water

The bittersweetness of the grapefruit makes me think of how it must have been for the people of Israel to drink the water that contained the gold from the melted idol. Drinking this "cup of gold" is a reminder that doing what the Lord has directed us to do is far more important than the approval of people around us.

2 pink grapefruit
peel from 1 grapefruit (optional)
2/3 cup pearl barley
1/2 cup sugar
water

Squeeze juice from grapefruit, strain, and set aside. Take the remaining peel from one grapefruit, slice into quarters, and with knife, remove remaining grapefruit and most of the white part of the rind.

Put barley into a saucepan, and cover with one cup cold water. Bring to a boil. Just as barley reaches the boiling point, remove from heat, drain, and rinse with cold water.

Return barley to large saucepan, add 10 cups cold water and the grapefruit peel, if desired, and bring to a boil again. Cover and simmer on medium heat for 1 hour, stirring occasionally so barley doesn't scorch.

Strain the liquid into a pitcher, discard barley and grapefruit peel. Stir sugar into barley water until sugar is dissolved. Allow mixture to cool 1 hour.

Add juice from the grapefruit to the sweetened barley water. Refrigerate until well chilled; serve over ice if desired.

(Note: For an afternoon tea, the buttery flavor of shortbread or butter cookies is a lovely accompaniment to this drink.)

Celebrating:
SIMPLE TRUST

*N̄ow there is in Jerusalem by the Sheep Gate a pool,
which is called in Hebrew, Bethesda, having five porches.
In these lay a great multitude of sick people, blind, lame,
paralyzed, waiting for the moving of the water.
. . . Whoever stepped in first, after the stirring of the
water, was made well of whatever disease he had. Now a
certain man was there who had an infirmity thirty-eight
years. When Jesus saw him lying there, and knew that he
already had been in that condition a long time, He said
to him, "Do you want to be made well?"
The sick man answered Him, "Sir, I have no man to put
me into the pool when the water is stirred up; but while I
am coming, another steps down before me."
Jesus said to him, "Rise, take up your bed and walk."
And immediately the man was made well,
took up his bed, and walked.*

FROM JOHN 5:2–14

*I*magine how excited the man must have been to be healed after waiting for so many years! He was so excited he even forgot to ask who it was who made him well. This man's willingness to trust impresses me.

How do you see yourself acting in that situation? I would probably have handled it entirely differently. Like a lot of people, I have a tendency to want to understand everything. I'm one of those people who asks why.

Picture the same scene if the man at the pool was a question-asker:

"Why do You want to help me?"

"Why should I be able to get up and walk just because You say so?"

"How do You know what afflicts me?"

"Will this be a permanent change, or will I be sick again soon?"

"Couldn't You just put me into the water the next time the angel comes?"

Curiosity can be the foundation for learning, or it can be such a nuisance that no one wants to deal with us. Thankfully, Christ is infinitely patient. We have an example of Christ's patience with doubts and questions when Thomas encounters Christ following the Resurrection. Even though Christ had compassion for Thomas and showed Thomas what he wanted to see, Jesus said, "Thomas, because you have seen Me, you have believed. Blessed are those who have not seen and yet have believed" (John 20:29).

There are many instances where Jesus healed people. One continuous theme is that it was their faith that made them well, not simply Jesus' power. Jesus told the woman who reached out to be healed that it was her faith that made her well. He healed the centurion's servant because of the man's faith. When the centurion said that he knew that Jesus needed only to say the word and his servant would be healed, Scripture tells us that Jesus was amazed at his faith and said, "I have not found such great faith, not even in Israel!" (Matt. 8:10). Christ certainly had the power to heal whomever He chose. He just seemed to choose those who had faith.

"Blessed are those who have not seen and yet have believed."

There is an old saying, "Ignorance is bliss." While it may be hard to see how being uninformed or simple can be "blissful," it isn't difficult to see that innocence and a lack of questioning can make our lives less complicated and give faith an opportunity to abound.

The popular film *Forrest Gump* illustrated just this principle. Forrest Gump was simpleminded, but his lack of guile and questioning enabled him to take the best life had to offer and not even see some of the worst in what he encountered. He lived life with the kind of childlikeness that Jesus said each of us should approach Him with.

While many of life's situations call for a certain amount of discernment and perhaps caution, in our dealings with our Lord, a simple trust can bring blessing beyond measure.

For more about the people Jesus healed, see:
- *Matthew 8:5–13   The centurion and his servant*
- *Mark 5:25–34   The woman who reached out to Christ*

Bath Buns

The Bath bun originated in the English town of Bath. Bath was popular for its mineral baths, which were believed to have a healing quality. This reminds me of the pool where Jesus made the man well. These buns can help us remember how valuable simple trust is to our Lord.

2 tbsp dry yeast
3/4 cup lukewarm milk
3 cups bread flour
1 tsp salt
1/3 cup extra-fine sugar
4 tbsp (1/2 stick) melted unsalted butter
2 eggs, beaten
1 tsp caraway seed
3/4 cup mixed, diced dried fruit or candied citrus peel
   (optional)
1 1/4 cups golden raisins (optional)

Topping:
1 egg, beaten
crushed sugar cubes

Mix yeast, milk, and 3/4 cup of the flour in a small bowl. Leave in a warm place until frothy, about 20 minutes.

In a large bowl, sift together the remaining 2 1/4 cups flour and the salt and sugar. Stir in melted butter, beaten eggs, caraway seeds, and fruit if desired. Add the yeast mixture and mix until a soft dough is formed.

Turn onto a lightly floured board and knead for about 10 minutes, until dough is smooth. Place in large buttered bowl and leave in a warm place for about an hour, until dough is about doubled in size. Knead again for 5 minutes. Divide dough into twelve to eighteen pieces (depending on whether you prefer large buns or small buns) and roll each piece into a bun shape. Place on baking tray and cover with an oiled plastic bag. Leave to rise for another 30 minutes or until doubled again.

Preheat oven to 375 degrees. Brush buns with beaten egg and sprinkle with the crushed sugar. Bake for 15 to 20 minutes, or until golden. Let cool. (Serve with butter and an almond-flavored tea.)

Celebrating:
THE LORD'S PROVISION

And when he [Elijah] came to the gate of the city, indeed a widow was there gathering sticks. And he called to her and said, . . . "Please bring me a morsel of bread in your hand."

So she said, "As the LORD your God lives, I do not have bread, only a handful of flour in a bin, and a little oil in a jar; and see, I am gathering a couple of sticks that I may go in and prepare it for myself and my son, that we may eat it, and die."

And Elijah said to her, "Do not fear; go and do as you have said, but make me a small cake from it first . . . and afterward make some for yourself and your son. For thus says the LORD God of Israel: 'The bin of flour shall not be used up, nor shall the jar of oil run dry, until the day the LORD sends rain on the earth.'". . . And she and he and her household ate for many days.

FROM 1 KINGS 17:8–24

The widow of Zarephath was not an Israelite woman. Notice how she refers to God as "the Lord *your* God." This woman did not worship the living God, but she was acquainted with who He was and saw that Elijah belonged to Him.

This is a precious story because it shows how the Lord's people can be used to save unbelievers, even as unbelievers can be used by God to accomplish His purposes and bring glory to Him.

Corrie ten Boom saw this type of provision firsthand during World War II. Corrie was a Dutch Christian who, along with her family, helped hide many Jews from the Nazis during the war. She and her family were arrested and spent time in various Nazi camps. At one point, she and her sister Betsie were imprisoned together at Ravensbruck, one of the worst Nazi death camps. The most remarkable aspect of their story is their constant faith in God and witness for Him, even in the midst of atrocious circumstances. God proved faithful to them during their captivity by answering prayers and meeting needs in miraculous ways.

The prisoners were not allowed to keep any personal possessions, but there were times when things slipped through. Friends that had been released tried to send things that would help them survive—a warm sweater, food, vitamins, small Bibles or portions of the Gospels.

Someone sent a small bottle of vitamin drops that Corrie worked hard to keep hidden. Betsie had never been in good health, and the terrible conditions of the camps only compounded her troubles. Even with her own difficulties, Betsie insisted on sharing the vitamins with others in need. Every evening, Corrie placed a drop of vitamins on the rations of bread of those who needed them. Corrie was concerned that they would run out and she would no longer have any for her dear sister, but Betsie would not hear of hoarding them. As the days passed, the line of those wanting the vitamins grew, but there was always enough to go around.

. . . even unbelievers can be used by God to accomplish His purposes and bring glory to Him.

One evening, one of the prisoners who was assigned to the hospital brought a stash of vitamins she had taken from the staff lounge. The women were excited over their unexpected good fortune, and Corrie decided she would put the vitamins away until the last of the drops was gone. That evening, as she began the nightly rationing of vitamins, for the first time, not a drop would come from the bottle! Once again, God had miraculously provided for His beloved children and for those to whom they ministered.[3]

Perhaps you remember tales of people who shared whatever they had during difficult times like the Depression or wartime, even though they didn't have much. Too often now we will share only if we feel we have something to spare.

It is important to remember that the Lord has promised to supply all our needs, even when someone else is in need of what little we have. Maybe He even wants to use a miracle to do it!

Crumpets

Crumpets are best described as a cross between a pancake and what we call an English muffin. They remind me of the woman with the "bottomless" jar of oil because they are simple to make and were originally baked on a griddle over an open flame, perhaps like the cakes the woman made for Elijah. Crumpets can be served as a reminder of how the Lord can make miraculous provision for us.

1 1/2 cups mixed lukewarm water and milk
1 package active dry yeast
1/2 tsp sugar
2 cups all-purpose flour
1 tsp salt

Add sugar to lukewarm milk/water mixture. Sprinkle yeast over the mixture and allow to dissolve. Stir, and set in warm place until frothy, about 10 minutes.

Sift flour and salt into bowl and make a well in the center. Pour in yeast mixture and mix to form smooth batter. Cover and set in warm place for 30 minutes, until batter has doubled in volume.

Heat buttered skillet over medium heat. Butter three or four crumpet or egg rings or round cookie cutters. (You can also use clean, empty tuna cans with the top and bottom removed.) Put rings onto griddle and drop 1 to 2 tablespoons of batter into each ring.

As bubbles begin to form on the surface and the bottoms of the crumpets begin to brown, remove rings and turn over with spatula. Cook until golden on both sides. Serve immediately with butter and jam.

Crumpets can also be refrigerated and served a day or two later. Simply toast before serving.

Any of your favorite teas will be well complemented by a fresh crumpet.

Celebrating:
THE FREEDOM OF AN OPEN HAND

*Then Moses answered and said, "But suppose they will
not believe me or listen to my voice; suppose they say,
'The LORD has not appeared to you.'"
So the LORD said to him, "What is that in your hand?"
He said, "A rod."
And He said, "Cast it on the ground." So he cast it on the
ground, and it became a serpent; and Moses fled from it.
Then the LORD said to Moses, "Reach out your hand and
take it by the tail" (and he reached out his hand and
caught it, and it became a rod in his hand), "that they
may believe that the LORD God of their fathers,
the God of Abraham, the God of Isaac,
and the God of Jacob, has appeared to you."*

FROM EXODUS 3–4

No one explains this scene more clearly than Ken Medema in his insightful anthem "Moses." In Ken's version, Moses' conversation with God goes like this:

"What's that in your hand, Moses?"
    "It's just a rod."
"Throw it down, Moses."
    "But Lord I . . ."
"Throw it down, Moses."
    "But . . ."
"Throw it down, Moses!"
Moses threw the rod on the ground,
    and the rod became a hissing snake.
Old Moses started running (maybe you'd run, maybe I'd run),
    he was running from a hissing snake.
Running scared of what God's gonna do,
    runnin' scared He'll get a hold of you.
And the Lord said, *"Stop! Pick it up, Moses, by the tail."*
"Lord, don't You know that You never pick up
    a hissing snake by the tail?"
"I said, pick it up, Moses."

What happened when Moses obeyed changed everything:

"Oh, God . . . it's a rod again, it's a rod again!"
"Do you know what it means, Moses?
    Do you know what I'm trying to say, Moses?
The Rod of Moses became the Rod of God.

With the Rod of God strike the rock and the water will come.
With the Rod of God part the waters of the sea.
With the Rod of God you can strike old Pharaoh dead,
With the Rod of God, you can set the people free."

The song goes on to ask one of the most significant questions I've ever encountered:

What do you hold in your hand today?
To what or to whom are you bound?
Are you willing to give it to God right now?
Give it up, let it go, throw it down.[4]

Has God ever asked you these questions?

Several years ago I was at one of those transition places in my life. The deep desire of my heart was to work with young people, but God seemed to be opening doors for me to help establish a Christian broadcasting system in Argentina.

I agonized over this opportunity for several days. *I* didn't want to work in broadcasting anymore. *I* didn't want to go overseas as a missionary. And if I was going overseas, *I* didn't want to go to South America.

I argued with God over it. I tried to convince God that working with youth was an honorable desire; God in turn asked, "Will you obey Me? Will you trust Me? Will you open your hand to Me and let Me have your dreams?"

This went on for several hours until I finally realized that more than I didn't want to go to Argentina or work in broadcasting, I *did* want to do what the Lord wanted me to do — even if that meant giving up my dreams of working with young people. The hard part was opening my hand and releasing the desires of my heart to God.

I believe God gave me my original desire because He had a plan all along. It's just that my desire couldn't be fulfilled until I allowed it to become God's.

What do you hold in your hand? Is it a goal or a dream? A relationship? A ministry? It's important to make sure we hold it with a hand open to God, knowing that the Lord may take it away to replace it with something else—and knowing, too, that maybe He just wants it to be "the Rod of God," giving it the power to accomplish great things for Him.

Cheese Straws

These twisty cheese crackers make me think of what Moses' rod might have looked like. Serve them as a symbol that whatever we release to God can be used in miraculous ways.

2 cups flour
pinch of salt
fresh ground pepper
1/2 cup (1 stick) butter, chilled
2 beaten eggs
2 cups grated cheddar cheese
paprika

Preheat oven to 400 degrees. Sift flour, salt, and pepper into a mixing bowl. With hands, rub butter into mixture until the mixture resembles coarse bread crumbs.

Add the eggs and cheese. Mix until it forms a stiff dough. (If dough is too sticky to handle, roll it into a ball, cover with waxed paper, and refrigerate for about 30 minutes.)

On a floured board, roll dough into a rectangle about 1/4 inch thick. Using a pizza cutter or sharp knife, cut dough into sticks about 1/2 inch wide and 6 inches long.

Brush each stick on one side with a little of the beaten egg and sprinkle with a little paprika. Twist each stick and place on ungreased baking sheets. Bake 8 to 10 minutes, until a light golden color. Cool on a wire rack. Store in an airtight container. (Enjoy the cheese straws with a cup of smoky Lapsang Souchong tea.)

Celebrating:
THE BLESSING OF GIVING

Honor the LORD with your possessions,
And with the firstfruits of all your increase;
So your barns will be filled with plenty,
And your vats will overflow with new wine.

PROVERBS 3:9–10

Scripture has much to say about honoring the Lord by giving back to Him a portion of what has been given to us. We know it's not because He needs what we have—He can have anything He wants at any time. I think what He wants to see is that we have a grateful heart and that while we know we don't deserve anything, we are thankful and want to serve Him with whatever He entrusts to us.

In the early days, God commanded the children of Israel to give offerings of thanksgiving and praise. He had to command them because in their sinful state, gratitude was not something that came naturally. It's the same for us. We have to be taught to be thankful. We have to be taught that we don't deserve the best of everything.

Have you ever observed children (or even worse, adults) who haven't ever learned that lesson? They tend to be selfish and greedy, not concerned with the welfare of others but always seeking the best for themselves. They aren't the type of people that most of us want to spend a lot of time with.

On the other hand, someone who has been taught to be grateful is gracious and caring and a joy to be around. When I was young, I remember reading *Highlights* magazine at the doctor's office. In each issue was an illustrated story about twin brothers, Gallant and Goofus. Gallant was kind and helpful and gracious and appreciative. His brother was selfish and sullen and obnoxious. The stories showed young children how much better it is to be a nice person than to be a brat.

The interesting thing about God's request that we honor Him with what is given to us is that there's a promise attached. If we honor the Lord with the best of what we have, our "barns will be filled with plenty." The first investment program—give to the Lord, and He'll repay with interest!

One man who took the Lord's promise seriously was R. G. LeTourneau, Christian businessman and inventor. His motto was, "Not how much of my money do I give to God, but how much of God's money do I keep for myself?" This attitude led him to give 98 percent of his income to Christian work. The assets of the foundation he established to disperse the money were valued in the millions during the 1950s—an uncommon amount during the postwar period.[5]

Since in today's world, most of us don't grow our own fruits and vegetables, we need to look at the "firstfruits" passages in a more figurative sense. What has God given you that you in turn can give Him the best of?

Maybe you have a home that could be used for youth activities or Bible study groups.

Do you have a minivan that could be used to pick up elderly people for church services?

Is there an evening during the week when the others in your household are busy that you could devote to discipling a younger woman?

Maybe you could teach a new wife to cook or sew—"home ec" classes aren't as common as they used to be, and many young people get through college on microwave popcorn, coffee, and pizza.

God gives to us that we may be stewards for Him. The more we have, the greater our opportunity to serve Him. He'll let us keep whatever He has given us, but it's best to reinvest it with Him. Then, as He promised, our "barns will be filled with plenty."

More about being a good steward can be found in the following passage:
Malachi 3:10–12.

Summer Pudding

Throughout Scripture we are reminded to honor the Lord with the first and the best of what we have. This dessert, filled with the best of summer's harvest, is a great visible reminder of that principle.

10 to 12 slices fine textured white bread
2 quarts mixed fresh fruit (or thawed frozen fruit)
2 cups sugar (1/4 cup for each cup of fruit)

Rinse fruit under cold water, remove any stems or unripe fruit, and drain well. Over low heat, mix fruit and sugar, gently stirring until sugar is dissolved and juice is formed. Set aside to cool.

Remove crusts from bread slices. Trim one piece into circle to fit bottom of 2-quart deep bowl or charlotte or pudding mold. Fit other slices of bread around sides of bowl, not overlapping but not leaving any gaps.

When fruit has cooled, spoon a little of the juice over bottom of mold. Carefully fill the mold with the fruit, and pour the rest of juice into the mold.

Cover top of fruit with remaining slices of bread cut to fit the bowl. Fit a flat plate or saucer inside top edge of mold, resting on the pudding. Place a heavy can or weight on top. Refrigerate overnight.

To unmold, carefully run a thin knife around the inside of the mold, and turn onto a serving plate. Slice and serve with lots of fresh whipped cream and more berries.

This is a refreshing dessert, great with any iced tea.

Celebrating:
THE MIRACLE OF FAITH

Then Joshua spoke to the LORD in the day when the
LORD delivered up the Amorites before the children of
Israel, and he said in the sight of Israel:
"Sun, stand still over Gibeon;
And Moon, in the Valley of Aijalon."
So the sun stood still,
And the moon stopped,
Till the people had revenge
Upon their enemies.
Is this not written in the Book of Jasher? So the sun stood
still in the midst of heaven, and did not hasten to go down
for about a whole day. And there has been no day like
that, before it or after it, that the LORD heeded the voice of
a man; for the LORD fought for Israel.

JOSHUA 10:12–14

*G*od is very concerned about the lives of His children—in the most literal sense. He is concerned about how we live and when we die, and if God has determined that there is a plan for us, no earthly enemy can prevent His will from being done.

Norwegian missionary to China Annie Skau Bernsten saw this truth demonstrated firsthand as she passed through a drought-stricken village on the way to a mission in the countryside.

As she and another missionary approached a small village, they found the villagers carrying idols and beating drums. As the villagers spotted the women, they came running, yelling that the women should remove their hats. The villagers were asking their gods to send rain, and they believed that if the gods saw dry grass on someone's head, they would be angry and send even more drought. The village needed rain soon or the whole year's crop would be lost.

Annie, standing six feet tall, fair-skinned and blonde, stood straight and told the leaders that she would not remove her hat to salute their idols. As the men lifted heavy sticks over their heads to kill her, she told them, "My God can give you rain; your idols cannot."

The men responded that they didn't know of any gods but their own and lifted the sticks again. Annie responded, "I promise you rain before midnight." Quite a thing to say with no sign of rain over the mountains!

The leader of the group convinced the others to let her go for now; but if this God she spoke of did not send rain, they would kill her.

The two women continued their journey and at last reached the small mission that evening. Annie related the story to the Christians there, and despite their concerns that she had promised something she couldn't deliver, Annie was confident that she would continue to live and minister in the country to which God had sent her.

Annie spent the rest of the evening on her knees in prayer alongside one of the Chinese believers. With a half hour left in the day, the door burst open and one of the others at the mission rushed in with the news that rain was coming and their lives were not in danger![6]

Just as God heeded the word of Joshua and caused the sun to stand still so that the Israelites had light to fight their battle, God heard the prayers of His servant Annie and sent rain to a place that hadn't had rain in weeks. Once again, God saved lives so that His work would continue and made it clear to those who saw the miracle that the living God is a mighty God, with power over heaven and earth and all of its elements. He alone is worthy of praise!

Scripture tells us that with just a little faith, we could tell the mountains to move into the sea. Now, maybe you don't need any mountains moved today. Maybe you like your mountains where they are. But perhaps you could use extra boldness to speak of the Lord to your coworkers. Or maybe you need strength to fight an injustice in your community or to stand up for quality education for your children.

Sometimes these very things can take a miracle. These miracles may not exist around every corner, but rather than limiting what God can do for us because we won't even ask Him for help, let's ask Him—believing—for the big things, and then watch what happens when He lets His power loose in our lives!

Sally Lunn Cakes

There is debate about the origin of this recipe. Some say that a young woman named Sally Lunn used to sell these cakes on the streets of Bath. Others say the recipe is actually an adaptation of a French recipe and "Sally Lunn" is simply an anglicization of "Sol-et-lune," French for "sun and moon." Either way, they represent God's ability to control even the very elements to see His purposes accomplished.

4 tbsp (1/2 stick) unsalted butter
3/4 cup milk
1 tsp sugar
1 package dry yeast
2 eggs, beaten
3 cups flour
1 tsp salt
1/2 cup sugar

Glaze:
3/4 cup powdered sugar
2 tsp lemon juice

Grease four large ovenproof custard dishes. Over low heat, melt butter with milk and 1 teaspoon sugar, stirring often. Add yeast and set in a warm place for about 10 minutes, until foamy. Beat in eggs.

Sift flour, salt, and remaining sugar together in a large bowl. Add yeast mixture, mixing well. Turn dough onto a floured board and knead for about 10 minutes. Divide into four pieces, shape into balls, and place in greased dishes. Cover and leave in a warm place to rise for about an hour.

Preheat oven to 450 degrees, and bake for 20 minutes, until golden brown. Stir lemon juice into powdered sugar until smooth. Remove cakes from pans and place on a wire rack to cool. Pour glaze over tops of cakes while still warm.

These cakes are good served hot with whipped cream or butter and·Earl Grey or English breakfast tea.

Celebrating:
THE FREEDOM OF FORGIVENESS

Then Joseph could not restrain himself before all those who stood by him, and he cried out, "Make everyone go out from me!" So no one stood with him while Joseph made himself known to his brothers. And Joseph said to his brothers, "Please come near to me." So they came near. Then he said: "I am Joseph your brother, whom you sold into Egypt. But now, do not therefore be grieved or angry with yourselves because you sold me here; for God sent me before you to preserve life. For these two years the famine has been in the land, and there are still five years in which there will be neither plowing nor harvesting. And God sent me before you to preserve a posterity for you in the earth, and to save your lives by a great deliverance. So now it was not you who sent me here, but God."

FROM GENESIS 45:1–8

*I*f this scene were to take place today, you can almost see Oprah and Phil and Geraldo fighting it out over which talk show Joseph and company would appear on first. Can't you see the heading in *TV Guide?* "Ricki Lake Show, Families who sold their brothers . . . and the brothers who saved them." Sadly, the real title of a recent show was "My family betrayed me . . . and I can't forgive them."

The truth is, the "can't" in these cases would be more accurately stated "won't." Scripture addresses what can happen to us when we won't forgive. A lack of forgiveness leads to bitterness, and bitterness to destruction. What most people don't realize is that it is not the object of the bitterness that is destroyed but the person who harbors the bitterness. Dr. S. I. McMillen wrote, "I am a slave to every man on whom I pour the vials of my wrath."

It's interesting that he uses the word *slave.* Joseph was actually a slave for a time, but his forgiving nature allowed him to be free even while in captivity. Even though his brothers had freedom, their inability to forgive Joseph for being Israel's favorite caused them to live in the bondage of guilt for many years.

A story of forgiveness that caught my attention recently was the report of a minister in Bridgeport, Connecticut, who performed a special wedding ceremony. In his address to the couple, the minister said, "Love means knowing that you can say, 'I'm sorry' and 'I forgive you.' *I'm sorry* and *I forgive you* are the key words in any relationship." The dramatic part of the story is that the groom had accidentally killed the son of the minister several years earlier.[7]

A lack of forgiveness leads to bitterness, and bitterness to destruction.

Accident or not, most of us would have a hard time forgiving in a situation like that. Some may say there had been forgiveness, but we would not likely choose to associate with the "guilty" party, let alone participate in such a personal and significant event.

In a way, it's an earthly example of a similar event that will take place some time in the future. We will be the bride, the guilty party responsible for killing the Son of God; Christ, the Bridegroom, who made the ultimate sacrifice by dying in our place. Our heavenly Father, with His unfathomable forgiveness, will accept us as the Bride of Christ and welcome us into His kingdom as His eternal family.

For more about Joseph and his family, see
  Genesis 37—46.
The Bible describes the marriage supper of the Lamb in
  Revelation 19:7–10.

Nutted Wild Rice

When Jacob sent his sons back to Egypt to buy grain, he instructed his sons to take some of the best fruit of the land as well as some honey and nuts as a gift to the ruler, Joseph. This dish is a symbol of the forgiveness Joseph offered to his brothers. The combination of the grains and fruit and nuts is symbolic of putting aside differences and coming together.

1 cup mixed long grain and wild rice
2 1/4 cups chicken broth (or equivalent amount water with
    2 chicken bouillon cubes)
1/2 tsp curry powder
1/3 cup toasted pecan or walnut pieces
1/3 cup toasted slivered almonds
1/3 cup diced, mixed dried fruit (peaches, apricots, apples,
    raisins, etc.)
3 tbsp butter

Bring chicken broth to rolling boil; add mixed rice and curry powder.

Return to boil, then reduce heat to medium, cover and simmer for 25 to 30 minutes. Add fruit and nuts and simmer about 10 minutes more or until liquid is absorbed and rice is tender.

Remove from heat, stir in butter, and let stand for 5 to 10 minutes. Fluff with fork before serving. This is a great dish to serve with chicken or turkey and any full-flavored tea.

For a light meal or brunch, an apricot-flavored tea enhances the fruit flavor of this dish.

Tea

Celebrations

for Special

Occasions

Celebrating:
EASTER

ℕow after the Sabbath, as the first day of the week began to dawn, Mary Magdalene and the other Mary came to see the tomb. And behold, there was a great earthquake; for an angel of the Lord descended from heaven, and came and rolled back the stone from the door, and sat on it. His countenance was like lightning, and his clothing as white as snow. And the guards shook for fear of him, and became like dead men.

But the angel answered and said to the women, "Do not be afraid, for I know that you seek Jesus who was crucified. He is not here; for He is risen, as He said. Come, see the place where the Lord lay. And go quickly and tell His disciples that He is risen from the dead, and indeed He is going before you into Galilee; there you will see Him. Behold, I have told you."

MATTHEW 28:1–8

*W*hat is the significance of this event? Have you ever considered how the Resurrection sets Christ apart from all other religious leaders and Christianity apart from other religions?

Other faiths recognize that they follow dead leaders. The most they can hope is to live a good life in honor of the men they have chosen as an example. In some religions it is a sign of great commitment to make a pilgrimage to the place where their religious leaders lived, died, and are buried.

The great hope of Christianity is that the tomb they placed our Lord in is empty. Jesus Christ conquered sin and death and walked into eternity as full of life as you and I. Actually, He was more full of life, since we are all in the process of dying and Christ rose never to die again. The significance of this is that we can have a living, active faith in a living, active Savior.

In his novel *A Skeleton in God's Closet*, Paul L. Maier creates a scenario of what it would mean to the world if Christ had not really resurrected. As the apostle Paul said in 1 Corinthians, "If in this life only we have hope in Christ, we are of all men the most pitiable" (15:19). Our faith is based upon the premise that because Christ was the sacrifice for our sins and He took the punishment of death for all of us, we now have the hope of eternal life following this life.

While the mind of man may have difficulty grasping this concept, the heart somehow knows the truth of the matter. Solomon wrote in Ecclesiastes that God "put eternity in their [the sons of men's] hearts" (3:11).

The story is told of Nikolai Bukharin, a Russian atheist, who was sent from Moscow to Kiev to address a huge anti-God assembly. He spent an hour chipping away at the Christian faith until it seemed that there was nothing left for a thinking person to believe in.

The great hope of Christianity is that the tomb they placed our Lord in is empty.

After a time, when the audience was invited to ask questions, a priest from the Orthodox church asked permission to speak. He faced the audience and greeted them with the traditional greeting, "Christ is risen." It is said that the entire crowd rose to its feet and responded as one, "He is risen indeed."[8]

No amount of logic or persuasive argument can take away the hope that God placed in each of our hearts—the hope that eternity does exist and each of us is to be a part of it. Resurrection Sunday is a time to remember and celebrate that Christ paved the way for us to spend eternity in worship and fellowship with our God.

Hot Cross Buns

This traditional bun is served either on Good Friday or Easter. I like it for Easter because it's a symbol of the empty cross and our Savior who defeated death to bring life to the world.

2 cups flour
2 tsp baking powder
1/8 tsp salt
1/2 cup (1 stick) butter
1/4 cup sugar
1/2 cup golden raisins
1/2 tsp ground ginger
1/2 tsp ground cloves
1/2 tsp ground cinnamon
1/2 tsp ground nutmeg
2 eggs

Glaze:
1 cup powdered sugar
1 tbsp milk
1/2 tsp vanilla

Sift together flour, baking powder, and salt. With hands, rub in butter until mixture resembles coarse bread crumbs. Add sugar, raisins, and spices. Mix in eggs and a little warm water, if needed, to form a stiff dough. Turn dough onto a lightly floured board, and knead gently until smooth. Divide dough and shape into buns.

Place on a greased baking tray, about 1 inch apart. Brush with a little egg or sugar and water for glossy tops. Score tops of buns in a cross shape with knife. Bake 20 to 30 minutes at 425 degrees, or until golden brown. Cool on wire rack.

Glaze: Mix ingredients together and stir until smooth. When buns are cooled, spoon icing into cross-shapes on buns.

This is another recipe that goes well with the citrusy taste of Earl Grey tea.

Celebrating:
VALENTINE'S DAY

Greater love has no one than this,
than to lay down one's life
for his friends.

But God demonstrates His own love toward us,
in that while we were still sinners,
Christ died for us.

JOHN 15:13; ROMANS 5:8

andlelight. Flowers. Lace. Chocolate. Valentine's Day. Do you get that warm, mushy feeling just thinking about it? I mean the big *it*—love. Volumes of books have been published, scores of songs sung, a plethora of poems penned in praise of love. Most of the love described in the songs and poems is about receiving love. A recent number-one song even claimed that the greatest love of all was found "inside of me." But isn't the greatest love a *giving* love?

There's a quote that says, "Love isn't love until you give it away." I think that's true. Love can't be appreciated or explored until it can be shared.

One of the most touching testimonies of love I've seen recently is that of Randall and Victoria (Ingram) Curlee. The California couple met two years before learning that Randall would die if he didn't receive a kidney transplant. This devastating news came just after the couple decided to marry.

Family members were tested, but none provided the kind of match needed for a successful transplant. Before Randall placed his name on the national transplant waiting list, knowing that doctors may not find a match before Randall's kidneys and other organs were severely damaged, Victoria was tested as a potential donor. In what doctors claim is the first case of its kind, the wife-to-be was able to donate a vital organ of her own to save her future husband's life.

The news media showed pictures of their wedding, which took place in the hospital the day before the surgery was to be performed. As the couple explained how they felt about what was about to happen, words seemed inadequate. Victoria was happy to offer this gift to a man she loved and wanted to spend the rest of her life with; Randall was overwhelmed by the gift. While the surgery was not without its risks, it was not too great a sacrifice for Victoria to give something like this to a man she loved who loved her in return.[9]

Most of us can imagine giving sacrificially to someone we love, especially if that person loves us back. But can you imagine giving your life for people who not only don't love you—they despise you?

Elisabeth Elliot Gren can tell you about this kind of love. It was this love that cost her husband Jim Elliot his life. He loved the Auca Indians of Ecuador enough to risk his life to bring them the gospel of Christ. The very people he went to save killed him and his fellow missionaries. This same love later took Elisabeth to the same village to live among the same people and continue the work that her husband had begun.[10] It's awesome to think of the forgiveness and sacrifice that took.

That's what Christ did for each of us. Even though He knew that many of us would never accept the gift of His love, He gave Himself that we could be forgiven and have fellowship with His Father.

Have you yet accepted the greatest gift of love ever given? Have you shared this gift with others in your life? I hope that Valentine's Day will always be a time to reflect on a love that reaches out to everyone.

When I was young, I received a small heart-shaped pendant as an award in a Sunday school contest. It has five, tiny heart-shaped pages: black, red, white, green, and gold. The black page is a reminder of our sin-filled hearts; red represents the blood of Christ that washes our hearts "white as snow"; the white page is our pure hearts; green represents spiritual growth as we read Scripture and pray; and the gold is a symbol of our eternal life in heaven.

(continued on next page)

78

Meringue Hearts with Raspberry Sauce

(continued from page 78)

This dessert reminds me of the message of that "wordless book": the snowy white of the meringue a symbol of our hearts washed clean; the deep red of the sauce a picture of the blood spilled as Christ's heart broke for the world He died to save.

2 to 4 large egg whites, room temperature
1 to 2 cups extra-fine granulated sugar (about 1/2 cup sugar
   per egg white)
Raspberry Sauce:
12 ounces fresh or frozen (thawed) raspberries
3 tbsp sugar
1 lemon

Preheat oven to 200 degrees. (If you have a gas stove with a pilot light, the pilot alone may be used.) In a clean glass or copper bowl, beat egg whites with a wire whisk or an electric mixer on medium speed until soft peaks form. Gently add sugar and beat until stiff and glossy.

To form hearts, use a heart-shaped cookie cutter to make imprints on a piece of foil cut to line baking sheets. Using a metal spoon or a pastry tube filled with meringue, draw heart shapes about 1/2 inch thick.

Place baking sheet into oven, allowing about 90 minutes for meringues to dry out. Be sure that they do not start to brown. Remove from oven and allow to cool completely before handling.

Sauce: Mix raspberries and sugar until sugar is dissolved. Press through fine mesh strainer or sieve to remove seeds. Squeeze lemon and strain the juice into raspberry sauce. Just before serving, fill well in center of plate with sauce, place meringue heart on top. Top with whipped cream, if desired.

Serve with rose-flavored tea.

Celebrating:
CHRISTMAS

*N*ow there were in the same country shepherds living
out in the fields, keeping watch over their flock by night.
And behold, an angel of the Lord stood before them, and
the glory of the Lord shone around them, and they were
greatly afraid. Then the angel said to them, "Do not be
afraid, for behold, I bring you good tidings of great joy
which will be to all people. For there is born to you this
day in the city of David a Savior, who is Christ the Lord.
And this will be the sign to you: You will find a Babe
wrapped in swaddling cloths, lying in a manger."

LUKE 2:8–12

*A*sk most retailers which single figure has the most significant impact on their business, and "Santa Claus" would probably be among the top five responses. It is, after all, jolly old St. Nick who gets credit for most of the giving that takes place during the Christmas season, when retailers make most of their money.

An unknown author penned a beloved poem that states that there is a man who is even more significant; in fact, he changed the world. The writer sums it up this way:

> Nineteen centuries have come and gone,
> and today He is the central figure of the human race.
> All the armies that ever marched,
> all the navies that ever sailed,
> all the parliaments that ever sat,
> and all the kings that ever reigned
> have not affected the life of man on this earth
> as much as that
> One Solitary Life.

The poem, of course, refers to the life of our Lord, Jesus Christ.

Unfortunately, in many cases, Christmas has turned from a time of rejoicing in the most generous gift ever offered to humankind to an occasion dedicated to greed. "Christmas" seems to have more to do with getting what we want than graciously receiving what is given.

One Christmas, my family learned a lesson about receiving gifts with a gracious heart from my niece Katie. As a six-year-old just learning to read, she was excited to practice by reading the tags and passing out all the gifts. She distributed everything under the tree until each person had a stack of gifts in front of them. As the only grandchild at the gathering, her stack had the most gifts, so she got to open a gift first. As Katie picked up the first gift to open, she read the tag and went and gave her grandmother a big hug. "Oh thank you, Grandma, thank you for my present."

"But Katie," said my mom, "you don't even know what it is yet."

"I know," she replied, "but I already know who it's from."

What a precious heart!

Katie, knowing her grandmother, knew that it would be a good gift even before she unwrapped it. Scripture points out in Luke, "If you then, being evil, know how to give good gifts to your children, how much more will your heavenly Father give the Holy Spirit to those who ask Him!" (11:13).

If only the world would learn to accept God's gift of love and forgiveness with the kind of trust and openness Katie showed. Often we want to check it out first and see what sort of strings are attached. After a while, we may decide we want it after all.

But a gift hasn't accomplished its purpose until it has been accepted by the person it is offered to. At Christmas, let's focus on graciously and gratefully receiving the gift our loving heavenly Father sent so many years ago.

More about Christ's birth can be found in the following passages:

- *Isaiah 9:6–7*
- *Matthew 1:18–2:12*

Christmas Cake

There are many versions of this traditional Christmas cake, similar to a fruitcake but not as dense. Substituting mixed dried fruit for the more traditional candied peel results in a mellower cake—more acceptable to those who don't care for traditional fruitcake.

1 cup raisins
1 cup golden raisins (or sultanas)
1 cup dried currants
3/4 cup mixed dried fruit
   (or 1/4 cup chopped candied
   fruit peel and 2/3 cup chopped
   candied cherries)
1 cup (2 sticks) butter

1 1/4 cups sugar
1 1/4 cups flour
1/2 tsp allspice
1/2 tsp nutmeg
1 tsp baking powder
1/2 tsp salt
4 eggs
1 cup chopped walnuts

Preheat oven to 300 degrees. Grease and flour an 8-inch springform pan. In a medium bowl, mix together fruits and toss together with 1/4 cup of the flour until fruits are evenly coated. Set aside.

In a large bowl, cream together butter and sugar until light and fluffy. Mix remaining flour, spices, baking powder, and salt together. Add a little flour mixture to creamed mixture, alternating with eggs one at a time. Beat well after each addition. Combine fruit and nuts. Add to batter a little at a time, mixing well.

Pour batter into prepared pan. Place pan on top of baking sheet to catch any drips. Bake in center of oven for 90 minutes or until tester comes out clean. Cool on wire rack before removing from pan. Sprinkle with sifted powdered sugar just before serving, if desired.

This cake is very good with a "Christmas Tea," usually some type of black tea combined with orange peel and spices.

Celebrating:
MOTHER'S DAY

I call to remembrance the genuine faith
that is in you, which dwelt first
in your grandmother Lois and your mother Eunice,
and I am persuaded is in you also.

2 TIMOTHY 1:5

One of the most beautiful examples in Scripture of a godly mother is Hannah, who wanted a child with her whole heart. The Bible says that "she was in bitterness of soul . . . and wept in anguish" (1 Sam. 1:10) as she prayed for many years for the Lord to give her a child. She finally told God that if He would allow her to be a mother, she would give her son to serve the Lord. The Lord honored her request and she gave birth to Samuel, who became a great prophet and was very instrumental during the years of the first kings in Israel. Because of Hannah's faithfulness, God also blessed her with three sons and two daughters after Samuel.

Scripture also contains many examples of women who were not good influences in the lives of their children. The important thing to realize is that, good or bad, a mother has a tremendous amount of influence, not only while children are young, but throughout their lives.

One of the "great" mothers of Christianity was Susanna Wesley. The wife of British preacher Samuel Wesley and mother of John and Charles Wesley, Susanna set an example for generations of women. She gave birth to nineteen children in nineteen years, although only ten of them lived beyond infancy. Even with that great number of children to raise, she dedicated time out of each day to spend with at least one child so that in the course of a week she had spent personal time with each of her children.

It has been noted that Susanna committed an hour each day, between six and seven o'clock in the evening, to read Scripture and pray. With all of the demands of her family, she made the time to set an example of dedication to Christ.

As her children grew, she invested time teaching her children literature and Scripture beyond what they studied in school. Her sons Charles and John were responsible for the Methodist movement in the Church of England, and their writings are still used in the church today. Charles in particular wrote a great number of hymns that continue to be sung in churches around the world some two hundred years after his death.[11]

What kind of spiritual legacy was left to you? I am fortunate to have a mother who committed herself to Christ as a young person and has spent her life growing to know Him and serve Him more. Throughout the years, in the midst of difficult family situations, many relocations, changing careers and ministry, my mom maintained her dedication to Christ and her commitment to raise us in a Christian environment. The patterns built into our family from before I can remember have helped me to maintain that commitment in my life as an adult.

There are many women in our churches or neighborhoods who haven't been so fortunate. Each of us has the opportunity to be that sort of influence in someone else's life. Our commitment to Christ can be a legacy for our children or for other young women who may be in need of that kind of example as well. Being a "spiritual" mother to someone can be just as important as being someone's biological mother. In fact, assisting with someone's spiritual growth can have eternal value far beyond that of their physical growth and nurture.

Has there been a spiritual mother in your life? Perhaps this Mother's Day celebration would be a good opportunity for you to let her know what she has meant in your life. May it also be a time for "you who are mature" to seek out someone to whom you can leave the legacy of your faith.

More about Hannah can be found in 1 Samuel, chapters 1 and 2.

Simnel Cake

In Victorian England, when young women were apprenticed to families, they were typically allowed only one day a year to return home to visit their own mothers. This day became "Mothering Sunday," and the young women would often bring this cake with them to show their domestic skills. It's nice to share this cake with someone who has given you a legacy to follow.

Cake:
1/2 cup flour
6 tbsp butter or margarine
1/3 cup sugar
2 eggs
1/2 cup golden raisins
1/2 cup currants
1/2 cup raisins
1/4 cup mixed, candied citrus peel or mixed, chopped dried fruit
1 tsp ground ginger
1 tsp ground cinnamon
1/4 tsp ground nutmeg
1 1/2 tsp baking powder
pinch of salt

Almond Paste:
1 cup powdered sugar
1 cup extra-fine granulated sugar
2 cups ground almonds
1/2 tsp vanilla extract
2 tbsp strained lemon juice
1 egg

Almond Paste: In a medium bowl, mix granulated sugar and ground almonds. Sift in powdered sugar. In another bowl, mix together vanilla, lemon juice, and egg. Pour half of mixture into dry ingredients and mix well. If too dry to form ball, add remaining liquid and mix until dough forms ball. Sprinkle sugar onto board and knead until smooth. Cover with plastic wrap and refrigerate until needed.

Cake: Preheat oven to 350 degrees. Grease and flour 8-inch round deep or springform cake pan. Divide the almond paste into thirds. Roll one piece into a 7 1/2-inch circle.

(continued on next page)

Cream together butter and sugar. Mix in eggs. Stir in fruit. Combine dry ingredients and add to mixture.

Put half of the batter into prepared pan. Lay the circle of almond paste on top. Fill pan with remaining batter, forming a well in center of batter so that the cake will rise level. Bake for 1 hour. Cool in pan for 5 minutes, then remove from the pan and allow to cool completely. Decorate by topping with another circle of almond paste. Crimp around the edges (like a pie crust). Roll rest of almond paste into balls and place around top of cake, using a little egg white to fix in place if needed. Return cake to 450 degree oven and brown almond paste for about 5 minutes.

Serve cooled with almond-flavored tea.

Notes

1. Hannah Hurnard, *Hind's Feet on High Places* (Wheaton, Ill.: Tyndale House, 1975).

2. Edith Deen, *Great Women of the Christian Faith* (Ulrichsville, Ohio: Barbour and Company, 1959).

3. Corrie ten Boom, John Sherrill, and Elizabeth Sherrill, *The Hiding Place* (Ulrichsville, Ohio: Barbour and Company, 1971).

4. Ken Medema, "Moses." Copyright 1974 Word Publishing. All rights reserved. Used by permission.

5. Dorothy C. Haskin, *Christians You Would Like to Know* (Grand Rapids, Mich.: Zondervan, 1954).

6. John D. Woodbridge, ed., *Ambassadors for Christ* (Chicago: Moody Press, 1994).

7. Associated Press, "At wedding of son's killer, pastor talks of forgiving," *San Luis Obispo County Telegram Tribune*, 14 November 1994, sec. B.

8. George Sweeting, ed., *Great Quotes and Illustrations* (Dallas, Word, 1985).

9. Associated Press, "Newlywed couple's kidney transplant a success at last," *San Luis Obispo County Telegram Tribune*, 10 November 1994, sec. D.

10. Elisabeth Elliot, *The Savage My Kinsman* (New York: Harper, 1957).

11. Arnold A. Dallimore, *Susanna Wesley* (Grand Rapids, Mich.: Baker House, 1993).

Bibliography

Augarde, Tony, ed. *The Oxford Dictionary of Modern Quotations*. New York: Oxford Univ. Press, 1991.

Bailey, Adrian. *The Cooking of the British Isles*. New York: Time-Life Books, 1969.

Cairns, Charlotte. *Tea Time Tips*. London: The Ettrick Press Ltd., n.d.

Garmey, Jane. *Great British Cooking: A Well-Kept Secret*. New York: Random House, 1981.

Kirshner, Sarah, ed. *Entertaining in the Victorian Style*. New York: Dutton Studio Books, 1990.

Lindemeyer, Nancy, ed. *The Charms of Tea*. New York: Hearst Books, 1991.

Loomis, Susan Hermann. *Farmhouse Cookbook*. New York: Workman Publishing, 1991.

Mackley, Lesley. *The Book of Afternoon Tea*. Los Angeles: HP Books, 1992.

Mashiter, Rosa. *A Little English Book of Teas*. Belfast, Ireland: The Appletree Press, 1989.

———. *A Little English Cookbook*. Belfast, Ireland: The Appletree Press, 1989.

Smith, Michael. *The Afternoon Tea Book*. New York: Collier Books, 1986.